Contents

1

where do I start?

Dedicated to my daughters, Rosanna and Shaunagh, and my wife Sarah, the Sleeping Lion.

Kevin Duncan worked in advertising and direct marketing for twenty years. For the last ten years he has worked on his own as a business adviser, marketing expert and author. He advises various businesses as a non-executive director, business strategist and trainer.

kevinduncan@expertadvice.co.uk
expertadviceonline.com

Also by Kevin Duncan:
Business Greatest Hits
Marketing Greatest Hits
Run Your Own Business
Small Business Survival
So What?
Start
Tick Achieve

People do talk a lot of nonsense these days, particularly in business. Don't let this be you. Woolly thinking will give you and your business a false start, and self-deception at this stage will lead to trouble later. When looking at your start up costs, don't take the view that you'll see how it goes. Work out what you need and make sure you can afford it. Write down on one sheet what you want to earn, how many sales at what price will be needed to achieve it, deduct all costs, and see if the plan works. Don't paralyse your launch by constantly reworking the figures. Get out and about. Meet socially and in a business context. Let people know what you do and that you are available for work. People can't use you if they don't know you are there.

It's a daunting prospect, isn't it? An empty desk, no customers, no confirmed money coming in, and no one to gossip with. Welcome to running your own business. Every issue is now yours to wrestle with, and yours alone. But then so is all the satisfaction when things go well, whether that is mental or financial. So let's dive straight in and work out how you are going to turn what many would regard as an ordeal into a fantastic success.

1 Assume that you have something to offer

Let's start by assuming that there is a market for your talents, otherwise you wouldn't have got this far. We have to believe that this is true otherwise you probably wouldn't be reading this book. By now you will have established the basics in your mind. Your thought pattern will have been something along the lines of:

* I am good at what I do.
* There is a market for my product/service. (Whether this is actually true and how you set about proving it to yourself will come later.)
* I can do it better on my own than in my current set-up.
* I have a way of doing it that people will like.
* What I put in and what I get out will be a better balanced equation than my current state of affairs.

That should just about cover it. Thousands of people go through this basic thought process at some point in their working lives – sometimes on many occasions. However, even if you have been able to tick all the boxes so far, the issue that you have to grapple with next is far more fundamental:

If I ran my own business, I'm not sure if I could live with myself.

What do people mean when they say this? Well, first, there are important issues with regard to exactly where you are going to do your work. What are your domestic arrangements? Could they possibly accommodate you achieving everything that you need to without disrupting all the other aspects of your life?

Second, there is your frame of mind: are you cut out to operate outside of a conventional work environment? Could you cope without the interaction? Could you motivate yourself when no one is there to give you a kick-start?

Evidence suggests that the majority of people are very capable of working on their own. They simply need a little guidance and encouragement to point them in the right direction. If you don't make the leap, you'll never know, so let's make a start.

It is essential that you feel good about yourself. You must genuinely believe that you can offer something of value to others, otherwise you would not have taken the plunge to set up on your own, or even be toying with the idea. Make this vital assumption and start from there. Don't be apologetic about your skills, either to yourself or to a potential customer. State them clearly, get used to saying them out loud, and become comfortable with explaining them to others. Without being arrogant, everyone who works on their own has to have a certain level of self-confidence. You no longer have colleagues to witness your performance and help you with encouraging observations. You rarely get debriefed objectively on how something has gone. Consequently, you have to be very adept at self-assessment. Now all the motivation has to come from within.

2 Be honest with yourself

Do remember, however, that confidence can be misplaced. In fact, over-confidence could beguile you into believing that you have a viable idea or a pleasant way of doing things when you don't. Confront your own hubris and work it out privately before it trips you up.

You work for yourself now, so you don't have to pretend about anything. In truth, you mustn't ever stray into the realms of fantasy because you would only be fooling yourself if you did. From now on it is your job to be sensible and realistic. Do not exaggerate your potential or delude yourself that you can do all sorts of things that you cannot. Equally, do not be sheepish about your skills. You will need to get used to showing a fascinating blend of confidence and humility. It is perfectly fine to have a different external persona, but make sure that you are honest with yourself and that you know your true self.

Consider your position with extreme care and as much objectivity as you can muster. Ask yourself:

* What are you good at?
* How much is that worth to someone else?
* How much will someone pay for what you have to offer?
* Is that enough for you to live on, or to satisfy your ambitions?

Get a piece of paper. Write down what you want to do in your business. Consider it for a while, and then decide whether anyone else would agree with you. This is the beginning of establishing whether there is indeed a market for what you do. Go for a walk. When you return, look at your piece of paper again. Is it any good? Is it nonsense? If so, write a new one. Stick it on the wall and live with it for a few days. Does it still make sense? Is it rubbish? Does everyone else claim the same thing? What's so different about the way that you would run your business?

These early enquiries are really important. They are the starting point of you being able to have a board meeting with yourself. A degree of schizophrenia here is essential. One half of your mind needs to be capable of putting forward an idea, and the other half needs to be smart enough to confirm or reject it without upsetting yourself in the process. That's no easy matter. So practise debating things on your own, weighing up the pros and cons, reaching a sensible conclusion, deciding what to do next, and remaining calm and objective throughout the whole process.

3 Research your market thoroughly

If you think you have an excellent idea, the first essential thing to do is to research your market thoroughly. Actually it isn't simply one thing to do – it's a lot of things. Try asking yourself these sorts of questions:

* What demand is there for what you provide?
* If you are producing a product, who wants to buy it?
* If you are providing a service, who needs it?
* Who else in the area does this already? (This could be geographical or sector-based.)
* Are they a success? If so, why?
* Are they a failure? If so, what does that tell you?
* What price can you put on your product or service?
* Does that represent a going concern or will you be hard-pushed to make a living?
* What outside factors are you subject to?
* Can you influence these factors or are you totally at their mercy?
* If you have no control over them, does that make the whole venture too vulnerable?
* If you were someone else, would you honestly embark on this venture?
* Why?

The questions are endless, but one of the best pieces of advice here is to be like an inquisitive child and always ask 'Why?' three times in relation to every question. Or, if you are inclined to overstate the potential of everything because you are so enthusiastic about it, ask someone else to ask you 'Why?' in relation to all your assertions about how this venture is definitely going to be a roaring success from day one. There is absolutely nothing wrong with oodles of enthusiasm at this stage. Actually, it is an essential prerequisite if you are to be a solo success, but the business won't succeed on enthusiasm alone if it is not tempered with some good old-fashioned realism. If you are a hopeless dreamer, get the reality mongers in to check if you are heading off on a wild goose chase that could end in disaster. This will soon establish whether or not you are deluding yourself.

With the advent of seemingly endless online data sources, a huge amount can be gleaned from just sitting at your desk and letting the information pour in to your desktop. In one respect this is fine, and it is a good place to start. However, do make sure that you get out and about and talk to people. There is no substitute for talking to prospective customers, wandering about a locality, and getting a human feel for things. Strike a balance between the two.

4 Work out how much money you need

This sounds obvious, but it is amazing how many people don't really cover the groundwork in this area. What is required here is not a forest of spreadsheets – just a really clear impression of how your business will work financially. Put simply, there are three types of money that you will need:

1 Investment at the start.
2 Monthly cash flow.
3 The profit (monthly or annual).

It is extraordinary how many businesses mess all this up. Here is the layperson's guide to the three types.

Initial investment

Let's look at the investment needed at the start.

* Do you need to put any money in at all at the beginning? Pause on this one for a moment. If the answer is no, then don't do it.
* If you do need to borrow from some other source, what demands will the lenders make on getting it back? Banks want interest. Investors want cash back. They don't lend money out of kindness. It is so easy to be seduced by the sort of macho talk that goes with establishing a business. You know the sort of stuff: 'We've got some seed corn investment from a consortium of city backers', 'The Venture Capital guys are really interested in the idea'. This may make you feel very important, but these people want their money back, and some. And they may want to be involved

in the way you run the business. Therefore, if you can do it without them, then do.

* If you do have to put money in yourself, when are you going to get it back? Don't delude yourself by excluding this amount from your assessment of whether the business is going to be a success.

Many self-employed people say that their business is 'successful' whilst simultaneously failing to remind themselves that 'the business' owes them thousands. This may be acceptable in the early stages, but not if there is no likelihood of you being repaid in the foreseeable future.

Monthly cash flow

This is the amount of income you need each month. Write down what you need. Now write down what you think you can get. Then build in time delays for late payment in the early days. This becomes your first cash-flow projection.

This projection has to be very, very realistic. You must have a reasonable level of confidence that it is achievable otherwise you will have a disaster on your hands almost immediately. You need to distinguish very carefully between income and profit. If you are ever tempted to start calling this income money 'profit', it has all gone wrong. That means it has gone wrong both on paper and in your head. To repeat, this is not profit – it is income. You can have an infinite amount of the stuff and yet still be making a whopping loss. Make sure that you make proper allowance for all the outgoings that may crop up, as well as an amount to pay yourself a salary to keep the wolf from the door.

Another massive pitfall is if you mentally earmark this money to 'mortgage' other costs. In the same way that shopaholics rationalize a purchase by saying 'I didn't spend £300 on that, so I can use it for something else', you must never double-count your money.

Calculate how much you need to make each month. Once you write it down, it is more likely to happen. (This is a general principle that works for almost everything – if you write it down, it is more likely to happen.) You can have a sensible minimum and maximum, but it is better if you have just one figure. Now you have to work out where it's coming from. Write down a realistic list of the value of your income in the first three months. If this turns out to be nonsense, write a more realistic list next time. As you become better at predicting, you will naturally build in time lags to reflect slow decision making and slow payment.

The profit (monthly or annual)

The final thing to consider is the profit margin. Ask yourself:
* How much is the profit?
* Does it vary depending on what you have sold?
* Does it vary by month or season?
* Does it fluctuate wildly?
* Why?
* What would make it more consistent?
* What would make it higher?
* What are the tolerance levels?
* What is the average target?
* Is that realistic?
* Is it good enough for you?

You need to keep a regular and close eye on this. You also need to have decided whether you need the profit margin monthly, annually or over any other time period.

* If you need the profit margin monthly, does this mean that your business plan does not include an amount for your own salary?
* If so, is that wise or realistic?
* If you can take the profit annually, how are you keeping tabs on the surplus that is (hopefully) building up?
* Can you equate it back to the running monthly amount?

Be aware that if you manage to convince yourself that you can wait quite a long time to realize a certain margin (a year or more), then you may well have a vulnerable business on your hands. Successful businesses make a good margin with almost everything they do, effectively from day one. Consider this carefully. There is no point in driving yourself into the ground all year only to make a few per cent, unless you are extremely happy with the figure that it generates.

The overall rule is to keep all this incredibly simple. The moment you overcomplicate the finances you will lose the plot and probably start talking nonsense about the business which, as we are beginning to realize, is one of the worst enemies of anyone working on their own. For another perspective on this whole area, have a look at one of my other books, *Start*, which includes a one-page business plan.

5 *Write a simple, realistic plan*

Quite a few diligent sole traders write endless business plans before they start, and there is nothing fundamentally wrong with that. However, a lot of them get so involved in the spreadsheets and the financial projections that they lose sight of the basics. The best business plans can often be written on the back of an envelope, usually in your local café or bar. Try this simple process:

* Write JFMAMJJASOND along the top of the page to represent the 12 months of the year.
* Now cross out at least one or two of them because you will be taking some holiday, and in the first year the whole thing will probably grind to a halt when you are not around.
* Now write a figure under each month to determine your income.
* Put the likely costs under each.
* Subtract one from the other and see what you have left.
* If you want to be particularly cautious, try crossing out the first three months' income because businesses always take longer to get off the ground than you think.
* Come back to your plan and ask yourself again: 'Is this realistic?'

This exercise will tell you something more fundamental than a meeting with the bank or your accountant. It will be a big surprise if you are happy with it first time. In truth, if you are, you should be a little suspicious. Live with it for a while. Try again. Make refinements (not on a spreadsheet, just in pen on another envelope). The great joy with this is that, by keeping it simple, you are now able to explain your business plan to anyone who will listen – and that includes you. Consequently, you are less likely to drift away from your main purpose as the months and years pass by. In some business circles, they call this 'focus'. You should call it 'knowing what I am doing'.

J	F	M	A	M	J	J	A	S	O	N	D
	X Launch date										
		X Hols					X Hols				
Income			4	4	4	4	0	4	4	4	0
Costs			2	2	2	2	2	2	2	2	2
Profit			2	2	2	2	−2	2	2	2	−2
First year profit: 10											
Pessimistic profit assuming no income in first 3 months: 4											

A simple plan.

Now, assuming that you have concluded that you do indeed have a going concern, there are some things that you will need to get under way.

6 *Invest in a distinctive identity*

You need to look good. Your company, shop or service needs a memorable name, a good logo, high quality headed paper, good quality signage, and business cards that invoke a reaction. The name may well be your own if you are known in your field. If not, choose something distinctive. Avoid bland sets of initials that no one can remember (such as BLTWP), or hugely cumbersome stacks of names like Jones, Duncan, Taylor, Hatstand European

Consolidated & Partners. They are not memorable and they imply a lack of clarity on your part.

Every detail counts. Don't skimp on quality of paper or thickness of business cards. Thin business cards are as weak as a limp handshake. Don't have them printed at a booth in a railway station! Check the spelling and punctuation really carefully on everything you produce. These days, the world appears to be one large typographical error. Don't be part of it.

What many business people don't seem to realize is that, if there are mistakes in the way that you market your own business, many potential customers will conclude that they should not bother to do business with you. They will automatically assume that what you offer will be as shoddy as your marketing materials, and, of course, they may be right. This is not an image you want to convey.

When you are describing your business, don't tell people that you haven't really made your mind up about what you want to do, or that you are 'just giving it a go to see what happens'. If you are indecisive about your own concern, you may well unwittingly give the impression that you will be indecisive or unreliable when dealing with your customers. And why would anyone want to do business with someone who has already said that they might not be around for very long? Customers are much more likely to be loyal to businesses that are reliable and consistent in their own right.

7 Get connected

Computers are an essential element of almost every business. They are not there to ruin your life, but to make it easier. If the nature of your business is particularly artistic, or if you simply don't like computers, then you may find the whole area quite daunting. But it is essential that you get your act together at the outset otherwise you will have real problems later.

You will certainly need a computer that is dedicated solely to your business. If you mix it with your social stuff then something will go pop very quickly. I have heard of people's kids erasing business databases inadvertently. You may well want a hand-held personal organizer to complement your mobile phone, or a combined device. Approach this cautiously though. If you are receiving messages throughout the evening and cannot resist looking at them, then your relationship with your partner will suffer horribly. For a full appraisal of these dangers and how to cope with them, read another of my books, *Tick Achieve*.

You really only need 'enough' technology to be efficient and professional. Carry the personal organizer at all times during the working day so that you can give instant responses about your availability. Don't say: '*I'll get back to you.*' Tell them immediately when you can meet or complete some work, and agree it on the spot. This is an essential self-employed version of the 'Think Do' management principle in which you must do something the moment you think of it. The last thing you need when you run your own business is a list of people to get back to. Do it now. It saves doing everything twice, and it makes you seem really on the ball.

Put all your information on your personal organizer and computer, and back them up regularly on disk to avoid calamity. (Put these back-up reminders in your diary now.) Think carefully about what you want your computer to do for your business, and choose your system accordingly.

* What information might you want to retrieve at some point in the future?
* What might your customers want to know?
* What might you want to know?
* What about your accountant or the dreaded tax inspector?
* What is the best way of cataloguing your records?
* What is the simplest way of doing all this?

Do not design your system around what the technology can do. Instead, decide what you want, and design something around those needs. Some careful thought at this stage could save you hours of heartache in the future.

8 Appoint a good accountant

There are whole books on this one subject, but let's stick to the basics. You really do need to know how to arrange all your financial affairs from the beginning. You won't want to discover at the end of the year that you have been recording information in the wrong way and that you now have to reorganize everything. Decide what you need, and organize all your money matters in the easiest possible way. Meeting your accountant once a year should be sufficient, with a few telephone calls every now and then to clarify any details. Keep it simple and think ahead. If you have money problems looming, address them early. Never succumb to the terrible practice of shoving bills in a problem drawer and ignoring them for months – you will create mounting debt and establish a reputation for not paying your suppliers. This is the slippery slope to bankruptcy.

Depending on the nature of your business, here are some of the gritty financial issues that must be addressed right at the beginning.

* Will you be a sole trader or will you register as a company at Companies House?
* Do you need separate bank accounts?
* If so, how many?
* How will your tax affairs be arranged?
* What type of National Insurance will you have to pay?
* Which elements of the business need to be kept financially separate?
* Do you need to rearrange parts of your current personal money habits to adjust to the new set-up?
* Do you need to register for VAT (value added tax)?
* What is the optimum system for paying the lowest amount of tax?

These fundamental questions need to be answered straightaway. Lots of people who work for themselves have started their first year without paying enough attention to these financial basics. At the end of their first trading year, they are then confronted by a nightmare of interrelated money matters that either cannot be undone, or cost a lot to disentangle. It is worth putting the work in now to avoid disappointment and unnecessary work in a year's time. There are many books on how to approach the technical detail, but the best thing to do is to have a frank meeting with the people who know about these things and then do exactly what they recommend before you start to generate any income.

9 Work out the materials you need

You need to work out precisely what materials you need to run your business. This sounds rather basic but you would be surprised by the number of people who drift into their new solo life without really knuckling down to resolve such basic questions as:

* If you are running a retail outlet, what stock do you need?
* How much investment does that involve?
* How quickly can you re-order?
* Do you know where from?
* Do you have the contacts?
* Where will stock be stored?
* Is it safe and secure?
* Is it insured?
* What system will you have for knowing when you are running out of stock?
* Are there legal requirements that you need to take into account?

If you are selling a service, at a minimum you will need a clear description of what you are offering cogently written down. This might be a brochure, your CV, a client list, some examples of your skills, and a list of things that could be of interest to a potential customer. You will certainly need terms of business. Most businesses start without these, and only draw some up after their first debt. The smart person has them from the beginning to set a precedent and to head off financial problems from the off.

We will look at some of the most important general business tools in Chapter 3 ('Getting the money right'), but there may be some specific to your line of work that you can work out for yourself. Here is a basic checklist:

* Description of your business
* Your CV
* Your clients
* Examples of what you offer
* Examples of what you have done for others
* Prices
* Terms of business.

Whatever they are, get them organized now.

10 *Network constantly without being irritating*

What's the difference between networking and marketing? Not that much. As a start-up business, you are unlikely to have the funds to pay for an advertising campaign or other publicity. The main burden of letting people know that you are open for business falls on you. Thus, you need to overcome any shyness or reservations you may have about marketing your business.

Have business cards on you all the time, including during social time. This is where you will pick up lots of your work. Once you start chatting, most people are interested in what you do. Without forcing your product or service on them, you can always seem professional by letting them know what you offer and having your contact details to hand. There is a huge difference between basic marketing and being irritating. Calm, professional marketers state what they do in a clear, charming way. If the reaction of the other person is reasonably positive, they might hand over a card. It's amazing how, months later, the phone can ring and a potential new customer says 'I met you once and now I have a need for what you do ...'

This is a vital hurdle to overcome, particularly if you have a shy or reticent nature. Who do you think will be the better client?

The one you cold-called and had a rather earnest meeting with? Or the one you met socially who decides to give you business in their own time? Speculative business meetings are no more scientific than interviews. They are based mainly on intuition. Yet if you already know you can get on socially with someone, or that they have a little insight into your private life, the chemistry part of the equation is already in place.

A final word on social media and social networking. There are businesses where this can be very appropriate, and used as an excellent tool to promote contact, discussion and possibly business. However, it is easy to fall into the trap of twittering on your computer all day and strangely discovering that you haven't got anything done, met anybody in person, or done any business. Try to keep this in perspective. Whilst everybody else is pursuing the latest fad, make sure that you are still talking to people, having meetings, and interacting with the real, rather than just the virtual, world.

11 *Now make it happen*

You are now as ready as you will ever be to start your new working life. Take a little pause and reflect on all the elements you have organized:

* Have you thought of everything?
* Have you been rigorous with the issues?
* Have you been completely honest with yourself?
  (If the answer is no, you need to have a serious word with yourself because you cannot run your own business if you delude yourself.)

Do you have the energy and determination to see this thing through? (Bear in mind that you may need more resourcefulness than you think because there will always be something that you haven't thought of to trip you up.)

It is also very important to remember that, if you don't do it, it won't get done. Sitting around doing endless Venn diagrams and spreadsheets won't pay the bills. Ideas that work in theory but not

in practice are not worth pursuing when you work on your own. As the old academic joke goes:

Yes, I know it works in practice, but does it work in theory?

Time is money. It's down to you and you alone. Scary? Certainly. Exciting? Absolutely.

So if you really want an answer to the question 'Where do I start?' the answer is: 'Right here, right now'.

Flashback

* Assume that you have something to offer.
* Be honest with yourself.
* Research your market thoroughly.
* Work out how much money you need.
* Write a simple, realistic plan.
* Invest in a distinctive identity.
* Get connected.
* Appoint a good accountant.
* Work out the materials you need.
* Network constantly without being irritating.

It is very important for any one to gather the prior experience before start a business. For example if you do not have the prior experience you have the chance to lose the business. But if you have some experi -ences you can gain your business.

the right tools for the job

Your contact list immediately tells you whether you know enough people to make your business a success. Your new business hit list lets you know whether you have a sufficient pipeline to ensure future sales. If you don't know *who* you know, or who you *want* to know, then you can't get going. Work out your ideal customer base. Your first customers will come from this list. If you don't tell them, they'll never know. Just because someone didn't buy your first suggestion doesn't mean they won't buy your second. Things change all the time. Bright ideas appropriately suggested are always interesting to people. There is no substitute for meeting, talking, and suggesting ideas. That's how you'll get your customers. If you cancel a new business meeting – for any reason – you may never get the meeting back in the diary.

It would be impossible for one book to cover everything that every business needs to get launched. However, we can certainly put some essentials in place. At base level, it will be you who instinctively knows what you need in order to start your business, that is to say the tangible items such as systems, stock, premises, materials, and so on. With a little thought you can work out your computer software, how often you review the essentials, when to have meetings with your suppliers and business associates, and so forth. What you may not have considered in such detail are the less tangible items – the approaches and disciplines that you need to motivate yourself to get things done.

It is very much a theme of this book that the simpler things are, the better they work. So in defining the right tools for the job, no attempt is made to persuade you to embark on any complicated systems or processes. In fact, the more complicated a system is, the less likely you are to get the job done. Here are the three sure-fire elements you need in order to generate a pipeline of initial business that will get you successfully launched, and enable you to keep business coming in when you have so much else to do all day.

These three really important tools will make your business a success:

Your most important tools

1 The contact list.
2 The new business hit list.
3 The telephone.

That's it. This is deliberately minimalist so there is no chance of you being distracted by massive spreadsheets with endless data on them. You don't want anything in the mix that wastes your time. There are many business people, and indeed consultants, who will try to convince you that you need various complicated systems to fuel your business plan. Experience suggests otherwise. The more paperwork and databases you have, the more confusion you have in the way of getting the job done. Some people love to hide behind this sort of stuff, but it doesn't work. The size of your database doesn't matter. The number of hot leads does. Piles of printouts don't matter. Two or three well-executed phone calls do. Consequently, we are going to look at these three elements and have a go at getting them under way.

12 *Write out your contact list and new business hit list*

The contact list

* The contact list is your lifeblood, and should be examined almost every working day.
* Start the first draft of the list by writing down everyone you know with whom you could possibly do business, and with whom you could get in touch.
* Ideally, it should only have the name of the person, the company and the date you last made contact with them on it.
* Don't be tempted to add other information. It will only distract you from the simple matter of picking up the telephone.
* If you really do feel that you need more information, write it somewhere else. Do not be tempted to enhance the list with extraneous detail – it has no bearing on the likelihood of you making the call, organizing a meeting, or achieving the thing that needs to be done, it only blurs your ability to get on with the task in hand.
* Every time you speak to someone or meet up with them, write the date down and move their details to the top of the list.

* This becomes your ready-made recall system. When you do not have anything to do, look at the very bottom of the list to see who you haven't been in touch with for some time (see Chapter 6, section 67 'Have reserve plans for every day').
* Having this list basically means that you can never legitimately claim that you have nothing to do. If you ever actually find yourself believing that this is the case (very unlikely when you work on your own, but let's just suspend disbelief for the moment), then you simply go to the bottom of your contact list and call that person for a catch-up.
* If you fix a meeting or do get work as a result of that call, you might give yourself the afternoon off. That's down to you, because only you know whether you deserve it.

---

1 July

MEETINGS

Roger Hughes	Hughes & Taylor	Meet 9 Jul
Matt Nicholls	Kaleidoscope	Meet 10 Jul
Sarah Taylor	Cool Corporation	Meet 15 Jul

DONE

Julie Manders	BFJW	Met 30 Jun
Andy Vines	Z Consortium	Spoke 28 Jun
Dave Jones	Zing Agency	Met 22 Jun

PESTER LINE

| Rachel Davis | Mayor Management | Spoke 23 May |
| Dave Bryanston | Ball & Associates | Met 6 May |

Example contact list.

* After some months have elapsed, draw a Pester Line at
  a certain date when you believe it is appropriate to call
  the client again. If you call more than once a month, you
  are probably pestering, but the appropriate frequency will
  depend on the nature of your business. Every six months
  is likely to be ideal in a service business where you are
  involved in one or two projects a year. But if you leave it a
  year, many of them will have left the company or changed
  their job description. Work out a frequency of contact that
  suits the nature of your business, and adjust it if it doesn't
  seem to be working.

When you call a client, always say when you last spoke or
met. They will be impressed by your efficiency. If you have judged
the frequency right, the most likely reaction will be 'Wow, was it
that long ago?' This proves that your call is timely, that it is not
pestering, and that it represents an appropriate 'keep in touch'
exercise.

If the client says call back on a certain date, then write the date
in your personal organizer immediately, and then do it exactly when
you said you would. This level of efficiency confirms that, if you do
end up working for them, you will definitely deliver what you say.

The number of people on your contact list needs constant
scrutiny. If there are more than 500 on the list at the outset, you are
either fooling yourself or spreading yourself too thinly. It is much
better to have a smaller number of viable, genuine prospects than a
huge list full of people you don't really know.

Keep a constant eye on your frequency of contact. If you
overdo it, after a period of receiving your (perhaps unwanted)
solicitations, you will begin to tarnish your reputation (in other
words, you will have overstepped the Pester Line). Or you will
simply dissipate too much of your time on people who aren't
interested in what you have to offer.

On the other hand, if there are fewer than 100 contacts on
the list at the outset, your business may not be viable. If you were
honest with yourself in Chapter 1, then you should have judged this

correctly. You need a decent universe against which to apply the normal laws of probability. If you are utterly charmed, it is possible that you could sustain a living on five customers who give you precisely the amount of work that you want exactly when you need it. That's very unlikely, although it might just be feasible in a service industry where you have an established reputation that provides a ready-made flow of work.

Much more likely is a selection of potential clients who don't actually give you work despite regular promises; work which does eventually arrive but much later than you expected; projects which turn out to be much smaller than anticipated when they do eventually arrive; and so on. If you sell a product, you may to a certain degree be at the whim of various market forces, a series of random factors, and the possible effectiveness of whatever offers and promotions you decide to run. Therefore, it is better if you can generate your own pipeline to even out all these variations.

In the start-up phase of a service business, you are allowed to have only 50 contacts, but you will definitely need 100 within three months. It is also worth considering whether your founder customers will continue to be long-standing customers and, if so, for how long. You will soon conclude that some will fall away, leaving the onus on you to develop fresh contacts. Be careful to consider this issue early, otherwise by the time you spot it in the normal run of things, you will already need the new work, and you will be dismayed by the time lag until new work materializes.

One of the most common laments of people working on their own is 'I'm too busy servicing existing customers to find new ones.' What feels like only moments later, the existing customers have moved on, and that person may well be out of business. Under no circumstances let this happen to you. It is your responsibility to become adept at running existing relationships whilst simultaneously engineering new ones (see point 21). You are a plate spinner, a dextrous juggler, and a one-man band all rolled into one.

Scary but true: if you cannot generate 50 genuine contacts in the start-up phase of a service business, you should not be working on your own.

The new business hit list

Your second essential tool is the new business hit list. This is the list that you generate once your contact list has taken shape. You need to think carefully and very broadly about anyone who could have a bearing on the success of your business. This is not a cynical exercise in exploitation. It is merely casting the net as wide as possible to make the most of the potential contacts that you have.

13 *Write down everyone you want to get in touch with*

Take your time. This list will not appear as if by magic. You need to rack your brains a bit.

* Don't think only of the one person you know at a company.
* What about colleagues, bosses and assistants?
* Would approaching several be more advantageous than only one?
* Have you considered friends with interesting jobs?
* Have you reviewed categories where you have related experience?
* Have you scoured the trade press?
* Have you remembered all your past colleagues who have moved on to other things?
* Think a long way back (you may surprise yourself).
* Have you included those who are still at your former places of work?

As a rule of thumb, the majority of people on this list should be people that you do not know, whereas by definition those on the contact list will be known to you, if only initially via a phone conversation.

14 Put the phone number by every one of your contacts

This may sound pedantic but human nature will dictate that if the phone number isn't by the name, it simply gives you another excuse not to make the call. You will soon realize that, when you work for yourself, making excuses is the highest form of personal insult. You are basically saying that you are happy to let yourself get away with it. Well don't! If the number is by the name, you have no excuse. Now make the calls (see Chapter 5, 'Taming the telephone').

15 Do everything when you think of it, otherwise nothing will happen

This is another fantastic truism, but it really does work. Think about it. Things either are or they aren't. Have you made the call or not? When you think of something, then do it immediately. 'Think Do' is one of the most fundamental principles of the successful businessperson. Of course, you cannot do literally everything at once, but what you can do is write down everything that needs to be done in a sensible order and work your way

NAME	COMPANY	LAST SPOKE	NUMBER
PRIORITY			
Dave Jenks	Zebra	11 Oct	7234 0001
Sarah Bowen	HHZ	24 Oct	7654 9870
Richard Stokes	Fruit!	31 Oct	7222 0987
NEXT UP			
Roger Batty	RB Cleaners	10 Aug	8675 4321
Bob Hatton	Standard	8 July	8970 5647
Mary Brooks	Dragon Design	1 June	7664 7865

Example new business hit list.

through it. Writing something down is in itself a doing action that helps to get things done. (For more on this, look at another of my books, *Tick Achieve*.) The great advantage that you have here is that in an office other members of staff keep interrupting you. If you are on your own, these interruptions are far less frequent so you can get a great deal more done. Ten phone calls in less than an hour? No problem.

16 *Constantly review the new business hit list to see if you are being realistic*

There is no merit in generating a vast list of prospects to call only to make yourself feel good when, in truth, you are unlikely to get round to calling them all, or might not get through to many of them, let alone get work as a result. Refine your thinking regularly by asking direct questions:

* Where are you likely to have most success?
* Why is a certain approach not working?
* What new approach might work?
* How can you apply one set of skills to another market?
* Have you overlooked an obvious source of business?
* What type of work do you enjoy most?
* Where do you make the best margin?
* Which examples of previous work are most impressive?

Now start getting the list into some sort of priority order. Put the hottest prospects at the top and revise the order when things change.

17 *Keep the numbers manageable*

Any fewer than ten numbers on your hit list and you are being lazy. How long does it take to make ten phone calls? Less than an hour, which of course means that you cannot claim that you don't have the time. Any more than 50 and you will faze yourself and do nothing, rather like facing a plate with too much food on it. If you have trouble tackling a list of this size, break it down into manageable chunks that suit you. Groups of six or ten, perhaps. Try colour-coding them so that you can distinguish one set from the other.

And if your first system doesn't work, simply admit it and invent a new one. Remember, any system is entirely for your own convenience and you don't have to discuss it with anyone else. Just make it work for you.

18 Keep inventing new ideas for contacting someone

You need to be vigilant about issues and trends. Pick up on articles in the trade press. Track movements of people and ideas. It works well when you ring up and say that you have noticed something relevant to them and have a suggestion. It shows that you are on the ball, and makes it easier to get work.

If you are selling products, keep re-analysing their appeal to your customer base.

* What is 'in' at the moment?
* Do your products fit that mood?
* Can you extend your range?
* What if you run a promotion?
* What if you alter your pricing?
* How about some local marketing?
* Are your marketing materials out of date or looking a little tired?
* Are there any seasonal events that you should be capitalizing on?

19 *Every time you get through to someone, move them to your contact list*

The definition of a contact is a meeting or a proper phone conversation. At bare minimum you will have explained who you are, provided your details and discussed the possibility of work at some point in the future. Never have someone on your contact list who should be on your new business hit list. This would be deluding yourself. They are not a genuine contact until you have spoken to them properly or met them and discussed at least the vague possibility of working together at some point in the future.

20 *Try to have 20–30 meetings fixed for the next 4–6 weeks*

In the early days, you need to pull out all the stops to generate some critical mass. That means a lot of meetings and probably a lot of coffee. Keep the meetings short and get to the point. You are a busy person and so are they. Never book more than four half-hour meetings in a day. You will lose energy and become bored of describing what you do. Two a day is ideal. Later on, when you have some paying customers, you can reduce this number and be more choosy. But to start with, there is no substitute for putting in the hard work.

The mathematics of this is discussed in more detail in Chapter 5, 'Taming the telephone', but the basics are as follows:
* The amount of business you think you currently have probably won't be enough.
* Something unexpected will happen, so you need contingency income.

* The law of averages will ensure that you will only get a percentage of the business you are aiming for.
* So you need to work out your strike rate.
* The number of contacts you need in order to fuel your business will be significantly greater than the number of customers or projects that you actually need to run a viable business.
* You have to overcompensate, particularly in the start-up phase.

21 Never cancel a new business meeting because you are 'too busy'

I'm sorry, I can't make it because I have too much on.

This is a classic mistake that many people make. If you think about it carefully, you will realize that the person you are talking to could make a number of assumptions. If you are incredibly lucky, they will be impressed that you are so much in demand. But the more likely reaction is that you are a one-man band who is unable to cope. Which means that you certainly won't be able to handle whatever they might have in mind. Goodbye project! You may never get the meeting again, so you should say 'yes', and work harder for a brief period.

The telephone

The telephone is the third essential string to your bow, and we are going to get to grips with it in Chapter 5 ('Taming the telephone'). If you have a particular issue with 'cold-calling' or any other aspect of phoning people, you might want to read that chapter now. If not, don't worry for the moment. It's not nearly as daunting as you may think. Meanwhile, assuming that you have successfully established your two lists, you have the right tools for the job and you are ready to do business.

Flashback

* Write out your contact list and new business hit list.
* Write down everyone you want to get in touch with.
* Put the phone number by every one of them.
* Do everything when you think of it.
* Constantly review the list to see if you are being realistic.
* Keep the numbers manageable.
* Keep inventing new ideas for contacting someone.
* Every time you get through to someone, move them to your contact list.
* Try to have 20–30 meetings fixed for the next 4–6 weeks.
* Never cancel a new business meeting because you are 'too busy'.

3

getting the money right

If you are working properly, the numbers will take care of themselves. Work out a rough shape of what the business requires, and then get on with it. Can you offer something that relies purely on your skill or experience? Start by thinking of the simplest thing that people might pay you for, and that requires as little investment and resources as possible. Material products have price points that are easier for the customer to guess accurately. They won't mind paying a certain mark up, but there will be a limit. Services, however, can be priceless. If you cost a lot, then you must be good. Examine any market and you will find this to be true. People like paying for high quality goods and services. So look carefully at the equation between price and quality, and consider premium prices that are justified. Don't sell yourself cheap.

Whatever you do to make a living, and no matter how much you absolutely love it, there is no point in doing it unless you make a sensible amount of money for the effort you put in. You really owe it to yourself to get the money side of things right. So how exactly do we set about doing that?

22 Concentrate on the money, but don't become obsessed with it

The dreaded money. The filthy lucre. Yes, it's true. From now on, when you discuss money, it will not be in some abstract way based on a remote budget that was agreed by someone you have never met. It will be a highly personal matter. Have you ever noticed how company people talk about budgets, allocations and fiscals? They often adopt a rather blasé manner. They even say 'ten k' instead of 10,000! Once you have earned £10,000 entirely off your own bat, it is extremely unlikely that you will ever use the letter 'k' in that way again.

From now on, every time you discuss money it will all be your personal money, so you'd better start concentrating harder. It has been said that you don't really appreciate what running your own business means until you have experienced a bad debt, so it is essential that you become comfortable talking about money straightaway. If you don't, you will probably agree to produce unspecified amounts of work over unclear time periods, and in some instances you might not get paid at all.

Alternatively, you may consistently sell products at margins so low that your business will not be viable. Although this sounds incredibly obvious, huge numbers of businesspeople pursue a large volume of sales so that they can brag about the scale of their operation. They crow about turnover, but frequently they are barely making a profit. There is no merit whatsoever in rushing around all year creating things to do when you aren't actually making money. It doesn't make any sense. Therefore, address this by keeping a very close eye on your margin, and by constantly questioning why you are doing what you are doing (see Chapter 6, section 66 'Never do anything unless you know why you are doing it').

Having lived through a number of recessions, I am often asked how to cope in one. It is tough medicine, but for what it is worth, this is my approach:

Don't do gloomy

No one wants to listen to a moaner. The circumstances might be different, but you don't have to be miserable. If you are, you'll run out of clients and friends, fast. If possible, do not use the R word.

Don't invoke a higher power

Bad performers love a recession because they can claim it's nothing to do with their performance – it's the economy, apparently. Bad people are bad whatever the economy is doing.

You only need one girlfriend

Wandering about complaining that there is no work is like saying there are no women in your town. You only need one girlfriend or piece of work, so go and find it.

Good companies do the right things all the time

There is no difference between the things you should do in a recession versus what you should be doing in any other circumstances. If you have to ask what to do differently in a recession, then it's probably too late.

Sometimes things go up, and sometimes they go down

So what if the economy is difficult at a particular moment? What do you expect, perpetual good times? Your success is entirely in your own hands.

Nip into the gap

You need to be dexterous enough to nip into the gaps that other people miss. Three examples follow.

* **If they want to save cost:** Go for a one-off project. Forget retainers and sweep up what's left. They save money and you gain income.
* **If they have fired a lot of people:** Propose a cost-effective shot in the arm. The remaining staff will be low in morale and wondering if they are next. Suggest something that helps them out.
* **If their income has plummeted:** Then they need new selling angles, a renewed business effort, and galvanizing of the troops. Propose your versions of these.

Stop talking about it and get on with something constructive!

23 *Weigh up the Service v Product distinction*

It is extremely difficult to give general guidelines about how to handle money without distinguishing between service- and product-based businesses. If you produce or sell any form of product, then the basic equation of your business will be based on the cost of making or acquiring it in relation to the amount for which you sell it. That's your margin or, put another way, 'materials with mark-up'. These businesses are almost always less profitable than service businesses that can attribute an acceptable price for an idea or a thing done (unless the manufacturer of that product has such enormous economies of scale that the amount of cash coming in makes the point irrelevant).

Of course this is a sweeping generalization, but it stands to reason that it is usually easier for a potential customer to attribute a perceived value to a tangible item than it is to an intangible one. Moreover, services and ideas can often cost nothing other than your time and talent to create. Consequently, in theory the price of a service or idea is limitless, whereas that of an item probably has a limit beyond which the market is unlikely to go. Consider this principle in relation to your own business. Ask yourself:

* What level of mark-up will your customers accept?
* What can you do to make what you provide worth more?
* Do you have enough services on offer to increase your average margin?
* Is your pricing appropriate for what you provide?

24 Work out how to have a near-infinite margin

If you run a service business, you should consider resisting the temptation to have offices, a partner, a secretary and any other baggage. You may be able to operate without them. Before you tear off and spend a fortune on things that you may not actually need, look at these questions.

25 Consider the lucky seven money questions

The lucky seven money questions

1 Could you do without offices by working from home? ☐
2 If you cannot work from home, is there an elegant alternative? ☐
3 Could you operate without a formal business partner? ☐
4 Could you have fewer prescribed arrangements where you can bring contacts in as and when work dictates? ☐
5 Could you survive without delegating anything? ☐
6 With a little ingenuity and re-engineering, could you do everything you need yourself? ☐
7 Could you pay yourself less for a while? ☐

If the answer is 'yes' to all of these, you can have a near-infinite margin. Of course, there are always those who claim that the sociability and interaction provided by an office environment are essential to the way they work. Fair enough. But you can imitate the important elements of these circumstances in almost every way by having plenty of meetings, bouncing ideas off friends and having a decent social life. In fact, being self-employed should massively improve your social reliability. For once in your life, you have no silly commute and no boss forcing you to stay at the office, so you can have much more enterprising free time on your own terms. You will probably live longer and have fewer medical bills as well.

26 Try to avoid the most time-consuming business issue ever: other people

Ever heard of 'high maintenance' members of staff? This is because one of the most time-consuming issues in any business is other people. No one is suggesting that you become a hermit, and perhaps your business genuinely cannot function without a workforce. However, if you are working for yourself, you do at least have the option to consider structuring a business that minimizes the effect others can have on your fortunes. You owe it to yourself to consider whether there is any possibility that you could run your business without anyone else. If there is any chance that you might, it is a strongly recommended option. Why? Because when you are on your own you:

* Make clearer decisions
* Make faster decisions
* Do business in your own unique style
* Avoid having to deal with politics
* Do not have to feel guilty about relationships with colleagues
* Can experience a truly direct link between effort and reward.

27 *Try to sell what you do, not materials with a mark-up*

There are many other things that can make an enormous difference to your profitability. Your talents theoretically have a limitless price. That means that, within certain sensible parameters, you can charge what you want. Materials are finite and have an approximate known price, so they can usually be undercut by a competitor and thus decrease your margin. The smartest sole traders do not sell materials or any fixed price service. They sell experience and ideas. This is not a way to rip off customers – quite the opposite. The most powerful question you can ask is:

If I fix x, what is it worth to your business?

The answer to this question is quite fascinating. Some potential customers will not have the foresight to estimate (or, in their eyes, speculate wildly) what they might gain by engaging your services. In which case, they won't answer the question or will not be prepared to say that the answer might be quite a large figure. This means that they are either not a genuine potential customer or that they will be a penny-pinching bad one, which means that you should not be pursuing their business anyway.

An enlightened potential customer will rapidly be able to put a likely figure on what they stand to gain (or not lose) from your involvement, and they will be big enough to tell you the true amount. Once you get into honest conversations of this type, you can forge a direct link between your price and the customer benefit. After a number of similar conversations, you may well have enough evidence and confidence to double your prices.

28 *The price–quality equation: if you cost a lot, you must be good*

What do you deduce about two products of similar type, one of which costs £2,000 and the other £200? The more expensive is probably better made and so of higher quality. It may have a cachet or brand value to which potential buyers aspire. There is nothing wrong with it being more expensive, assuming that there are people who appreciate those qualities and are prepared to pay for it. No matter how disparaging one chooses to be about products and services that are 'expensive', one is eventually forced to admit that, one way or another, there must be a market for them otherwise they would not remain in their market.

In which case, what would you deduce about two people, one of whom commands a fee of £2,000 a day, and the other £200? The more expensive is likely to be more experienced and therefore of higher quality. This is self-fulfilling, because if they are not, then in a fairly short space of time they will not generate any repeat business, and will fail as a business reasonably quickly.

It may be something of a rhetorical question, but which of these two people would you rather be? Obviously it is a hypothetical example and the gap between the two figures doesn't really matter, but the principle probably does. Far too many people who work on their own undercharge for their services, and it is often a mystery why. Nervousness certainly plays a part. Lack of confidence contributes too. And many will claim that if they put their prices up, they will either lose or fail to gain work. But if you think it through carefully, you will pretty much always look enviously upon someone who is successful in a particular field and come to the following conclusion:

If they cost a lot, then they must be good

This is, of course, the reaction that you should aspire to invoke in your customers and competitors. Clearly there has to be an appropriate balance between price and delivery but, in the main, you should always place the maximum possible value on what you have to offer. If you are uncertain about what that value is, you need to test your pricing first. One of the lovely things about being self-employed is that you can effectively reinvent yourself and what you offer every day. If yesterday's formula didn't work, try another today. Now consider putting your prices up, and be

prepared to turn work down if customers want it too cheap.
Your central maxim should be:

Charge a premium price and do a great job

29 *Aim for 50 per cent repeat business within three years*

If this aim frightens you, there is something wrong with your ambitions. Do you expect your customers to be pleased with the work that you do? If the answer is yes, which it certainly should be, then you should expect further work in due course. If you are selling products, there is still a service element to what you do, and your objective must be to have your customers coming back. Even accounting for the random availability of projects, seasonal factors and the cyclical nature of certain markets, you should always aspire to get more business from at least half of your existing customers.

You should also track satisfied customers when they move house, move to new jobs or have a change of circumstances. Whatever has happened, they will be confronted by a whole new set of issues, many of which you may be able to address. In a service business in particular, it is important to go and have a coffee with people when they move. It is flattering for them, it gives you a flavour of their new set-up, and there is always something new to discuss.

Of course aiming for 50 per cent could be criticized as banal. Who in their right mind would aim for a percentage? It is merely a figure that will fluctuate anyway depending on the size and shape of the other elements in your business. What should make sense though are the parameters above and below which repeat purchase levels should not rise or fall. If you have 100 per cent repeat business, then the corollary is that you have no new business. This is not good. If you have no repeat business, then you would certainly be worried about the quality and value of what you produce and the long-term prospects for your business, if only judged by word of mouth recommendation and customer satisfaction. And if you had a fantastic run of new business, then you would not mind at all if your repeat percentage fell. Perhaps we should conclude that the percentage should be no lower than 30 per cent and no higher than 70 per cent in any given year.

30 *Don't be small-minded about money*

Think big. Remember that you will probably have to type all your own invoices and do your own VAT return, so don't waste time with bits and pieces that don't get you anywhere. When quoting and invoicing, stick to units of hundreds or thousands of pounds. It is difficult to generalize here, but the basic rule is not to mess about with small fractions that do not really add to your profit, but which infuriate you when doing the books. Keep it simple and round the figures up or down (preferably up) in order to get the job done quickly and efficiently. In some instances you may lose a little on price, and in others you may gain a little, but you will save hours of fiddling about with pounds and pence or dollars and cents.

This is an extension of the 'successful people buy in bulk' principle, and applies to anyone who works on their own. Successful business people buy in bulk so that they don't have to waste time perpetually buying individual small units of a given item. This applies to pretty much everything: paper, paper clips, printer cartridges, stamps, envelopes – that rather irritating list of stuff that has to be done but doesn't really seem to have a bearing on anything. Time-wasters (who are never successful working on their own) repeat the process mindlessly again and again, usually failing to notice that the time spent on constantly doing this is detracting from their ability to do much more rewarding and profitable things. Put another way: have you heard the one about the person who never got anything done because they kept writing out lists of 'Things to do'?

Expenses are a case in point. No matter what your business, do not be petty about expenses. If at all possible, you should never charge them to the customer. If appropriate, build a suitable margin into your prices to allow for any extra services that you would normally wish to provide them. In a service business, be generous and broad-minded. Buy the client lunch, and pay for your own travel. Simply get on with it in a way that befits a well-paid successful person.

There are plenty of examples in Chapter 6, 'How to conduct yourself', that give suggestions to help you along, but here is just one example. If you find yourself producing estimates for jobs that go into tiny detail and try to justify your every movement, you have probably either got the wrong pricing or the wrong type of customer. What a lot of people who work for themselves forget is that discussing the trivia takes as much time as talking about the important things. It therefore costs just as much money, but as a proportion of the value of the lower priced job, the time spent will probably not be viable. Therefore, be very careful not to become dragged into the mire of discussing tiny financial details whilst all the time you are missing the main point. If a customer becomes too uptight about a job and will not agree what you deem to be a fair and honest price for a job well done, walk away from the job. You are better than that.

Furthermore, don't forget that your accountant can make allowances for all sorts of things, and tidy up all the details at the end of the year. That's what you pay them for.

31 *Be canny about requests for free or 'win only' work*

'Share in our success or failure' was one of the worst traits of the dotcom boom in the late 1990s. This is a euphemism for 'I won't pay for anything unless things have gone really well and I decide that I can afford it.' The main rule is never to give anything away for free, unless you have an overwhelming reason to do so. When people ask why you won't do speculative work, the best answer is 'Because I don't need to'. They really have no response to that.

Although there is usually no reason to give your time away for free, you do of course reserve the right to charge less or provide free work if you deem that it is appropriate. You should try not to, but you are the best judge of any given state of affairs, and the joy of working on your own is that you do not have to discuss it with anyone else. Here are some possible reasons why you might want to provide something free or at a reduced price:

* Because it will lead to repeat business.
* Because it will lead to new business.
* Because it is part of a much bigger deal.
* Because they are a highly-valued customer.
* Because you can.

A final thought on free work. If you have had a really good year, why not offer to work free for a charity or a worthy cause for a limited period? Your expertise may be worth significantly more than any donation you might ordinarily make, and skills are often more useful than cash. No money needs to change hands, and you can add their name to your client list and use it as part of your sales patter.

32 Consider Everyday Flexible Pricing

Here's a slightly radical idea that is not for the faint-hearted: Everyday Flexible Pricing. Each day when you work on your own is effectively the beginning of a new financial year. You can state your prices any way you like, describe your background as you see fit, and accept or decline work on a whim. It really is entirely down to you. Which means you could double your prices tomorrow if you like.

This may or may not be a good idea in your market. However, you could certainly test two pricing levels side by side to see whether it has any bearing on the success of a deal. Or you could steadily increase your prices as your confidence, experience and flow of work increases. For example, if you are discussing a project that is very similar to one you have just done, increase the price by as much as you think suits, probably somewhere between

10 and 50 per cent. If the client accepts, then this becomes your new price for an exercise of that type.

Over time, this should fuel an ever-upward value equation for your business. One word of warning though: if you do try this, make absolutely sure that you know which prices you have quoted, and to whom, otherwise you may lose the plot and come across as though you are making it up as you go along. Which, of course, would be the truth.

Flashback

* Concentrate on the money, but do not become obsessed with it.
* Weigh up the Service v Product distinction.
* Work out how to have a near-infinite margin.
* Consider the lucky seven money questions.
* Try to avoid the most time-consuming issue ever: other people.
* Try to sell what you do, more so than materials with a mark up.
* Examine the price–quality equation: If you cost a lot, you must be good.
* Do not be small-minded about money.
* Be canny about requests for free or 'win only' work.
* Consider Everyday Flexible Pricing.

how to communicate effectively

What is the most appropriate medium to use to speak to a customer? Some careful thought will always lead to a better result. So think before you dive in. Broadly speaking, no one cares what you do to earn a living. It's your job to express it clearly so everyone can understand and, ideally, to make it interesting and appealing. If you can't, why should anyone else bother to try to understand it? Business CVs are dull. Which is more interesting: your work or leisure activities? There are probably many competitors who do exactly the same as you. The difference is you. So let them know what you would be like to work with. Get out and about, in both commercial and social contexts. Chat to lots of people. Ask lots of questions, stay open-minded about people and circumstances, and don't close off opportunities before they have a chance to develop.

Communication. This must surely be one of the most complicated issues in life, let alone in a business context. Where would we be without communication? Humans cannot exist without it. Almost everything we do involves the need for it. And yet often we really aren't very good at it. So let's have a look at some of the methods at our disposal, and work out how best to use them.

33 *Choose the right method of communicating*

Methods of communicating are constantly changing. Until relatively recently you could only really talk to someone in person, by telephone or by writing them a letter. That was about it. You might have faxed someone or sent a courier to speed things up a little. Then came the internet and mobile telephony, and the whole scene changed. We now require a much broader set of communication skills, and we need to put much more thought into what is the appropriate method for any particular situation. We can try to put these options into some sort of hierarchy. Here is a rank order of possible communication methods, based on (a) the likelihood of you being correctly understood and (b) probable sales success as a result:

1 Talking face to face
2 Telephone conversation
3 Letter
4 E-mail
5 Text message.

With regard to effectiveness, option number one must beat all the rest by a hundred to one. Consequently, if at all possible, only conduct your important business face to face. However, this is not an excuse for endorsing a 'meetings culture' in which legions of earnest businesspeople sit in meetings all day without really knowing why. Quite the opposite, in fact. It is perfectly feasible to conduct meetings in a brisk, polite way that acknowledges the fact that most people are busy. Come in, get to the point, agree what is to be done, and get out. Half an hour is the ideal length for a business meeting.

Having a good telephone conversation can also be highly productive. Nevertheless, there is a huge difference between a telephone conversation with someone you have not met in person as opposed to one with someone whom you can picture. Everything is easier if you have met, so if it is important, make sure that you do indeed meet. Have a look at Chapter 5 ('Taming the telephone') for all sorts of ways to make your phone conversations more pleasant.

Letter writing is next down the list, but a very long way behind. In the direct marketing industry, the average response rate to letters is around 2 per cent. It wouldn't be much use if you only got through to two out of every 100 of your prospects, so letters have to serve a very distinct purpose. If you know that the recipient likes to have things written down, then a letter makes sense. If you have done a lot of research into the potential reader and you have a carefully argued and quite bespoke proposal, then a letter may work, particularly if it is followed by an appropriately timed phone call.

And so we come to the dreaded e-mail. In many respects, this method has completely revolutionized our lives. Certainly, many people who work on their own could not succeed without it because of its fantastic ability to deliver things quickly and its power to enable them to stay in touch. The internet has also facilitated the transfer of much more information, and access to all sorts of data that would previously have been cumbersome and costly to obtain.

I have deliberately left off the main list social media, webinars, linked-in, twitter and all the other developments that are part of online communication. The reason for this is that, although they involve communication in the broad sense, they lack the specificity of a clear business sales channel. They are more conversational than directional, and need to be regarded with caution in case you find that you have spent all day chatting when you should have been selling or doing.

As a high quality communication method, e-mail leaves much to be desired. Why? Because:

* Anything you send can be totally ignored.
* The presentation style is mainly in the hands of the receiver, not you.
* Most messages are not checked, so that any errors can make you look unprofessional or ignorant.
* People you don't know about are sometimes blind copied on the original for political purposes that you know nothing about.
* Your original message or reply is often forwarded to someone you know nothing about.
* Response rates for e-mails have plummeted to the depths of junk mail – typically 2 per cent. So if you send 100 out, you may only get two replies.

The sort of chaos that can ensue from these possibilities shouldn't really require any further elaboration. Suffice it to say that any communication method that has these pitfalls needs to be treated with extreme caution. It is perfectly fine to bat e-mails back and forth with a known customer who likes the method, but otherwise it is unlikely to be the method by which you grow your business. E-user beware!

34 Become adept at describing what you do in less than 30 seconds

Lethologica is an inability to recall words. This is not something that you would ever want to suffer from. Now that you work on your own you need to improve your word power so that you are very proficient at explaining what you do. Potential customers may be interested for a maximum of one minute. This is true at an interview, a drinks party, in the pub, at the squash club – anywhere in fact. After that, they become bored. You need to get your act together and come across in a lucid, enthusiastic way.

Start by writing down what you do in no more than three sentences. Now read it out loud. Does it sound daft? If so, rewrite it. Try again. Does it sound like a cliché? Does it sound like all the other waffle you read in corporate brochures or hear from politicians on the television? If so, change it. Make it fun and engaging. Do it with some pride and a lot of energy. Excellent. Now you can use it for face-to-face conversations, telephone calls and all your written work. Also bear in mind that this should evolve constantly to keep pace with the manner in which your business develops.

35 Be prepared to improvise on the spot

Life's a mess. Make it up as you go along! One of the joys of running your own business is that you can change the rules any time you like – several times a day if you are feeling particularly mischievous. There's nothing more boring than someone who repeats the company mantra in a soulless manner, so go with the flow a little. If you spot an opportunity, try out a sales angle. If you have a random thought, say it. If you want to discuss an idea without necessarily proposing it, then do so. It's vibrant and fun.

36 Introduce some humanity into your CV

You've all seen the type of thing:

Relentlessly successful, moved from A to B to C, married with two children, enjoys theatre and music.

Thats the gist of the average CV. What can we deduce about this individual? Are they extremely reliable or just really boring? The best that we can guess is that they are a fairly steady individual. Let's compare them with the next one:

Gained experience doing X, transferred skills to different industry Y, broke away and set up on own doing Z, plays in a rock band, flies birds of prey at the weekends, amateur artist and occasional cartoonist.

Who would you prefer to have a drink with? Who would you rather do business with?

You get the idea. If you introduce some humanity into your business life, interesting things start to happen. First, you get to know your customers so much better, not because you are asking inane questions such as 'Did you have a good weekend?', but because you really get to know what they are up to, and in most cases people do some very interesting and enterprising things that they never mention unless you ask. Second, if you work in the type of business where it is appropriate to overlap your work and social life, the whole thing becomes a pleasure instead of a chore. Third, smart customers deduce very quickly that if you are enterprising in your spare time, you probably are in your working time as well. Finally, mentioning your hobbies and outside interests can give you that extra element of pride in your achievements that is crucial to anyone who works on their own. There's nothing wrong with drawing satisfaction from your hobbies as well as your work and transferring that confidence between the two whenever you need it.

37 Remember that people give business to those with whom they like having meetings

You need to acknowledge what meetings are for in the first place:

* To establish a relationship.
* To propose something.
* To agree something.

That's about it really, and unless anything is incredibly complicated, you should be able to do what is necessary in less than an hour, and preferably less. If you are the sort of person who waffles, who has meetings without really knowing why, who doesn't prepare, and who fails to bring new ideas and proposals with them, you will be quite tedious to have meetings with. This is not a favourable impression to create. You need to be really on the ball. Don't set up meetings for the sake of it. Always ask yourself: 'Whats the point?' Be sharp and lively, and establish a reputation as a person with whom a meeting is always a pleasure. You want your customers to be saying: 'Whenever I have a meeting with you I get something out of it.'

38 Meet lots of people and stay open-minded

Let's spend a moment or two discussing the difference between networking and meeting lots of people. Over time you can become quite good at working out the difference between the two. When you start out, you do actually need to meet quite a lot of people. This is because the law of averages proves that you need a reasonable critical mass of contacts to make any business work. In the early days, the shape of your business will not be sharply defined (no matter how rigorous you were in the planning stages), so you need to stay open-minded.

Moreover, bear in mind that every meeting you have involves a judgement of character as well as an assessment of someone's technical skills. The more people you communicate with, the more experience you will have of working out whether you will get on well with them, and whether they will be relevant to your aspirations for your business. Once you have met, you need to keep a close eye on what happens next. Try asking yourself these types of questions:

* Did they send through the thing that they said they would in the meeting?
* Did they call in two weeks' time as they promised?
* Did they give my details to their colleague as we agreed?
* Did they consider my proposal and give me a response?

If the answer to any of these is 'yes', you may be on to a decent working relationship. If the answer is mainly 'no', you need to consider carefully whether the person is a time-waster or someone who usually fails to do what they say they will. If this proves to be the case, they will not be fulfilling to do business with and, if they are an associate of any kind, be aware that their poor approach will reflect badly on you.

Once you have met a number of people, you can refine your approach into some proper networking. This is not a cynical process whereby you extract all the benefits from people and give them nothing back. In some quarters, the very word 'networking' has as bad a reputation as 'Sales'. Properly executed networking should benefit everyone. Let's define the difference between meeting many people and networking. In the early days, you need to meet lots of people and stay open-minded. When you have built up some experience of their capabilities and your aspirations, you can network. This will involve keeping in contact with those who could benefit from your skills and vice versa, at a frequency that is appropriate to your line of work and how busy they are. You keep in touch, help them out, suggest things and, ideally, do business together. Everyone wins.

39 *Take your customers to lunch and insist on paying*

It could be lunch. It could be breakfast, dinner, the races or even just a drink. The details don't matter. The thing is that social surroundings promote a totally different mood than those of a meeting room, many of which appear to be designed precisely to reduce the chances of meetings being enjoyable. Suggesting a social get-together is a constructive, magnanimous thing to do. What does it say about you? It says that:

* You are broad-minded.
* You are interested in other aspects of your customers than their money.
* You can afford it.

Therefore, you will be engineering a situation in which you can show your generosity, your interest in the client, and quite possibly the degree to which you are on the ball with your suggestions of places to go and things to do.

What do you talk about when you meet up? A bit of business, certainly. But mainly simply ask short, open-ended questions and then shut up. You'll be amazed what comes up.

People will talk when they are put at ease. They will talk about their families and relationships, their concerns, their feelings about their job, sport, hobbies, current affairs – pretty much anything. Of course there are some bores in the world, but in the main there are interesting things to learn and discuss. The more ideas you have, the smarter you will appear, not because you are faking it but because it will be true. It's all part of honing good communication skills.

40 Rewrite all your marketing materials

Assuming that you do succeed in creating a dynamic environment for your business, things will probably change quite rapidly and so should the manner in which you describe what you do. The chances are that your marketing materials will become obsolete pretty quickly. So update them. It doesn't have to be an expensive exercise if you stick to the basics and concentrate on the elements that work well in your market.

Get out all the stuff that you have had done and spread it out on a large table. Ask yourself some questions:
* What do you think of the materials?
* Do they accurately represent what you do these days?
* Which bits worked and which didn't?
* What can you learn from that?
* Do you use some elements more than others?
* Has the emphasis of your business changed?
* Is there any point in producing something new?

41 Design a clever mailing to send to your customers

It's amazing the number of businesses that send out one launch mailing and then sit back thinking that they have 'done marketing'. Oh dear. The market is changing all the time. People come and go. Products and tastes change. You can never conclusively prove that something that didn't work before won't work now.

Consider the merits of sending out a new mailing to your customers:

* What would you say?
* Have you ever done it before?
* Did you learn anything?
* Who would you send it to?
* Existing customers for repeat purchase?
* Or new potential customers? If so, where will you get their details?

I use the word 'mailing' in its broadest context. Choose your medium carefully, as we discussed in section 33. You may choose to use different media for different messages. Whatever you do, don't just fire off an e-mail to all your contacts and assume that the business will roll in.

42 Ask your customers what else you could do for them

How many businesses plough on churning out the same old stuff, assuming that what they provide is what their customers want? Most people don't like change unless someone else does all the work and makes it a pleasure. Then they can opt in or out on their own whim and in their own time. Unfortunately, when you work on your own, that someone is you. It is your job to stay very close to your customers and the markets in which you operate.

When you have some new ideas that you want to test, or even if you have none at all (hopefully not, otherwise you may be lacking the entrepreneurial spirit shown by most

people who work on their own), talk to your customers.
Ask them:

* What else could I do for you?
* Did you realize that what I do for you is only a fraction of what I do for some of my other customers?
* How much does what I do make a difference to your business?
* What are the main things preoccupying you at the moment?
* Would you like me to investigate something new for you?
* Are you dissatisfied with any suppliers who provide similar services to me?
* Do you know any other potential customers who might want to use my services?
* What could I do better?

By now you will know that when you ask such open-ended questions, it is your job to shut up and pay attention. The new selling opportunities are always lurking in the answers given. Let the clients talk. In many instances, your customers will invent new work for you on the spot. Occasionally drop in new ideas. Offer to develop a thought into a proposal. Suggest that you do a little development work on a subject and call them next week to see if it is worth proceeding. In the modern business world they call this being proactive. In truth it is simply having ideas and getting things done.

Flashback

* Choose the right method of communicating.
* Become adept at describing what you do in less than 30 seconds.
* Be prepared to improvise on the spot.
* Introduce some humanity into your CV.
* Remember that people give business to those with whom they like having meetings.

* Meet lots of people and stay open-minded.
* Take your customers to lunch and insist on paying.
* Rewrite all your marketing materials.
* Design a clever mailing to send to your customers.
* Ask your customers what else you could do for them.

5

taming the telephone

Every time you make a call, you learn something. Their colleague's name, their mobile number, their daily pattern. It's all useful information. When you get through, you might even enjoy it. You might think it's cold, but the other person might not. 100 calls = 3 jobs. This equation might be wrong, but the principle isn't. So work out an appropriate ratio for the medium you are using. Disguising what you do behind impenetrable nonsense is the last bastion of the desperate. Become adept at describing what you do in less than 30 seconds. Get familiar with stating clearly and simply what your business does. If you waffle, they won't get it. Tell them that you know how to fix the problem because you are experienced. That's what they want to hear, and why you can charge them for doing it. Your expertise does not have to be wrapped up in complication.

The phone is a two-way machine that can be a great asset or an object that invokes considerable fear. Many people hate what they describe as 'cold-calling'. If you are one of them, and particularly if you are in a service business, you need to address this issue urgently and befriend your phone. Once you get the hang of it, it's really not as bad as you think.

With regard to the telephone, there are certain matters that anyone who runs their own business needs to confront. Start by reading this chapter and try to apply some of the suggestions. In particular scrutinize carefully 'The ten golden rules of unsolicited calling' on page 76. Whatever you do, don't reject the idea before you have a go – it is not nearly as onerous as many would have you believe.

43 *Don't call it 'cold-calling'*

Who said cold-calling was cold? Rarely has an activity been so badly titled. Calling someone on the phone is usually a very pleasant thing to do. Even in business. In reality, those who view it as cold-calling are probably cold themselves, and are not that keen on other people anyway. It is far better to view the whole process as just calling someone for a chat. The fact that you have never met that person has nothing to do with it. If you are charming and have something interesting to say, it will be a pleasure for both sides. You wouldn't hesitate to call a friend, and sometimes you might even call them without a reason. In business, there is always a reason, so all you have to do is state clearly what the reason is and get to the point.

There are many ideas here about how to get the conversation started and overcome the initial hurdles. However, they will work to a lesser degree until you get to grips with the emotional barriers and convince yourself that it really isn't such a big deal to pick up the phone, and that great things can happen once you take the plunge. One way to do this is to consider all the worst things that could possibly happen if things don't go as well as you hoped. Here are some examples:

They say they are not interested in what you do

So what? This is very valuable information. Lots of people spend weeks, months, years even, pursuing someone who simply isn't interested in what they have to offer, and never will be. This could be an individual or a company whose culture doesn't suit yours and vice versa. Take it on the chin and move on.

They refuse to take your call

This is most interesting. If someone spends the bulk of their time hiding behind a barrage of secretaries and assistants, there are two things you can deduce about them. Either they may be genuinely busy, or they enjoy creating the impression that they are busy. If it is the former, then it doesn't mean that they are not interested in what you do. Either keep trying or use a different method of getting in touch that suits their style better. If it is the latter, think carefully about whether you would really like to do business with them. Will they be a badly behaved customer? Will they respond to your calls if you do end up working together? Will they pay you on time? And there are a host of other issues that could make your life a misery. 'Only do business with people you like' is a maxim that will serve you well.

They are rude or dismissive

This is a bit unpleasant but no less helpful than either of the above. Rude people may well occupy influential positions for intermittent periods, but nobody enjoys working with them and, over time, the system spits them out. If you work on your own, there is absolutely no point in dealing with people of this type. They ruin your life and they do not deserve your contribution. Avoid them like the plague.

They never answer their landline

This may not be the end of the road. Most landlines contain a message that mentions the name of a colleague or a mobile number. This gives you another way in. Depending on the nature of the business and the person you are calling, you may feel that it is appropriate to call their mobile, or speak to the colleague in question. Your decision here may be aided by looking at their website to see whether their mobile numbers feature. If they do, you have clearance to proceed.

44 *Admit that the phone will never ring unless you market yourself*

Many people who set up on their own make the mistake of thinking that the phone will ring and provide them with work in the same way that it did when they were employed in a company. It doesn't. In fact, on some days, it doesn't ring at all. One or two extremely blessed individuals come out of corporate life and seem to have a charmed flow of ready-made work without appearing to have to market themselves. But one thing is for sure: it never lasts. In year two or three, these people are left adrift as that source of business fades.

Besides which, you may not even have a contact base from a former life. In this case, you need to market yourself from the outset, to a fairly broad audience. The first stepping stone in this process is admitting that the phone is unlikely to ring unless you make it do so. In other words, you need to create the momentum that makes people want to call you back, whether that is today or at some point in the future when they have a need for your product or service.

This is a very simple piece of logic. If you don't ask the guy out, he won't even know you are interested. If you don't call and express an interest, then potential customers won't consider you.

45 *If you make 100 calls, you will get 40 meetings, and three jobs*

The precise figures may vary depending on the nature of your business, but the essence of the equation never does. Take a moment to think about this. It stands to reason that you must generate a critical mass of interest in what you have to offer. The mathematics of it has nothing to do with the quality of you, your product or service, or your customer base. If you jot down all the possible reasons why someone does not want to do business with you this week, you will soon see how circumstances are more likely to stop work happening than to start it.

Start with these reasons why people will have no need for your services this week, and add your own:

* Holiday
* Illness
* Apathy
* Disorganization
* Budget change
* Colleague disagreeing
* Company politics
* A rival proposal
* Other priorities
* Haven't got round to it.

You could double the length of this list in less than a minute. That's without even entertaining genuine, overriding, business considerations such as price, quality, distribution, over-supplied markets or product specification. Once you think about it, it's a miracle that anything ever gets done at all.

Remember: 100 calls = 40 meetings = three jobs

This is why people keep talking about the 'pipeline' in a new business context. In truth, it is more helpful to see it as a funnel or hopper. The work appears to come sequentially in a linear way, but actually it only appears to be that way because, at any given moment, you have many contacts and proposals which, in all probability, will generate work at some point, but not necessarily now. It never happens all at once, and that is precisely why you need a regular flow of people who just might be interested in your offer in any given week or month.

When you run your own business, the moment you believe that you have a settled and steady customer base, everything may well be about to go wrong. Why? Because you will have failed to prime your next source of business to replace the business that you will inevitably lose soon, based purely on the law of averages. Some people claim that they fail to do this because they are too busy. This is a very poor excuse, particularly when you consider the huge irony of having too much time on your hands when you have lost a significant customer.

Perhaps another reason for not preparing is that you don't think it will happen to you because your quality is high and your relationship with your customers is good. That may well be true, but it has almost nothing to do with whether you will retain them or not. At some point, the law of averages will cause some factor you had not considered to jeopardize your business.

It may not be 'your fault', but it will certainly be 'your problem', so anticipate it and fix it before it is irretrievably broken.

46 Prepare your selling angles

Now let's get down to the business of what you are actually going to say on the phone. You've done the hard part: you've sat down with a list of people to call, researched all their numbers (see Chapter 2), and you've dialled. So what exactly are you going to say? You need to consider some selling angles:

* Who are you?
* What do you do?
* Why are you calling?
* What do you (or your business) offer?
* What has it got to do with them?

* What do you want to happen next?
* What happens if they are not there and someone else answers?

You need to work through all these possibilities before you call. Don't dial and then panic. If you have considered all the angles beforehand, you won't be caught on the hop.

Never leave a message

If you do, you immediately cede control of the contact to the other person. This means that, the moment you call again, you are pestering.

47 Don't use jargon to disguise what you do

So you have got through to the person you want to speak to. Stay calm. Remember that waffle and jargon are the last preserve of corporate behemoths. We all know that obscure phraseology is designed to confuse people so that it seems as though you need their services (and so that they can charge you more). But when you work on your own, the opposite is true. If they can't grasp what you do in one sentence, they won't bother to listen to the rest. Cut out the waffle and come straight to the point. If you are unfamiliar with the word 'obfuscation', look it up in the dictionary. It will say something like 'to make something unnecessarily difficult to understand'. This is the opposite of what you want to achieve.

Use clear, simple expressions to explain what you do and why you would like to do business with the potential client. Don't be vague about what you do – let them grasp it quickly and move the conversation on to the area that matters to you.

If you find this difficult, and you still sound vaguer than a vague thing, try some of these techniques:
* Pretend you are explaining it to your mother or father.
* Phrase it as though you were talking to your mate in the pub.
* Write it down and eliminate anything that sounds silly.

* Say it out loud and ask yourself whether you sound daft.
* Tape record it, listen back and decide if you would welcome such a phone call.
* Practise saying it in front of the mirror.
* Try it on the phone, then debrief yourself as to whether you sounded sensible – if not, draw up a new version.

But whatever you do, make sure you do all this before you call. It really is essential that you sound lucid and persuasive, and under no circumstances use a vital prospect as a guinea pig for a ham-fisted dry run that goes wrong. Get organized in advance and get it right. If you are dipping into this book there is more on this in Chapter 4.

48 *Tell them you are available*

There is a tendency in modern business to create the impression that you are always frantically busy. This is completely inappropriate for someone who runs their own business. You need to strike the right balance. For a start, people soon detect whether you always claim to be very busy, and they probably won't believe it is always true. Moreover, if you really are so incredibly busy, how will you fit in the proposed work for them? Think about it. You need to convey the impression that you would like their business, but that it is not essential that you have it today. Desperation does not work. Confidence and calmness does.

Another side effect of always appearing to be frantically busy is that there is a distinct possibility that you will convey the impression that you are disorganized as well. This is a poor signal to be sending out. There is a good balance to be found in always making yourself available for potential business, but on your own terms and in your own time (within reason). Obviously you do not wish to come across as indifferent, but you should reserve the right to pace the flow of any new business advances to make sure that you deliver appropriately for your existing customers, because they pay the bills. When you are talking on the phone, make it clear that you are available to do the necessary work.

49 *Try selling the opposite of everyone else*

It may seem fashionable to promote yourself or your business as specialists. Somehow people think it is more reassuring if they have a 'specialism', and to be fair there is some evidence that certain specialists are able to charge more for their services. Yet experienced business people can usually fix a whole range of issues, so it is important for you to think broadly. This is very likely to increase your opportunities, your income and the breadth of your work. This in turn will introduce greater variety to your work.

Of course, this suggestion presupposes that you are indeed capable of doing more than one type of thing. In theory it is possible that you genuinely cannot, but most people have more than one talent, and those who are capable of working on their own are certainly at the more enterprising end of the spectrum, and are usually used to fixing a range of problems. Give it some thought. Try portraying yourself as a generalist, not a specialist. You could get more work, and you will in all probability enjoy yourself more by venturing into new areas that you haven't tried before.

50 *Tell them it is simple (because you are experienced)*

Tugging your beard and saying that something is really complicated does not inspire confidence and is as dismaying as a plumber staring at your boiler and declaring 'We'll never get the parts for this.' By all means appear thoughtful and reflective. Tell them that you have dealt with a similar issue before and that you know what to do – particularly if this is the first time you have spoken on the phone. A lot of work is commissioned not because the customers cannot do it themselves, but because they do not have the time. Consequently, it is often appropriate to tell them that they could certainly do the work themselves, but would it help if you took it off their 'Things to do' list for a certain price? At this point, speed and convenience may become more relevant than your precise skill set.

51 *Offer to solve their issue quickly*

Doing something quickly doesn't mean that the work is bad quality or bad value. It may be precisely what the customer wants. As the old story goes, if a portrait costs £10,000, the painter is charging that for a lifetime's experience, regardless of whether he or she does the job in a day or a month. The speed with which you can do something has absolutely no bearing on the value. An experienced mechanic might diagnose and cure a problem in half an hour. An amateur might take all day, and may even do a poorer job of fixing it. The fast solution may actually be the higher quality one, assuming that the person in question knows exactly what they are doing.

This approach is also a pleasant counterpoint to suppliers who want to make a job last longer so that they can charge more. A good maxim for those who work on their own is:

Don't string it out in order to charge a higher price

Offer to fix something quickly based on the assumption that you are experienced enough to know what you are doing, and organized enough to schedule it in efficiently and get on with it. If it is a business issue that needs resolving, offer to do it as a commando raid in a reasonably short space of time (you will be able to judge the appropriate timing based on your intimate knowledge of your sector). If you do the job well, you will have a satisfied client, and you will have been paid a good price for a sensible outlay of time. In short, neither party will have wasted any time.

52 *Be ready with examples of customers for whom you work*

People love case histories, and when you catch them on the phone they don't usually have much time. They want easy anchor points on which to base their purchasing decision, just like references on a CV. They want to ask:

* Who else have you worked for?
* What did you do for them?
* Can I have some examples?

You need to anticipate these requests and, after a short while, you should be able to rattle these off effortlessly, even in your early days when you may actually be using examples from your previous corporate life. You do not always have to refer to something directly related to the task in hand, but you should become skilled at drawing on examples and making links between issues.

Customers do not always want people with direct experience of their field. Of course the narrow-minded ones might, but you wouldn't want them as customers anyway, now would you? Very often people in particular businesses have become too close to the issues that they encounter every day. This is something I call 'going native'. If they are smart enough to realize this, they will welcome a fresh perspective. That's where you come in. It is extremely likely that your skills are transferable and that they could benefit another business area if applied thoughtfully. So don't be sheepish about your skills – simply think broadly and suggest how your strengths could benefit the issue being discussed.

53 *Don't start discounting before you have even met*

Don't start discounting on the phone. Remember your central maxim from Chapter 3: 'Charge a premium price and do a great job'. State your rates clearly and without embarrassment. If they balk at the cost, say that you can discuss it when you meet and when you have better understood the nature of the possible work. Anyone who works on their own has examples of potential clients who have exclaimed 'How much?!', only to come back later with their tail between their legs having had a poor experience elsewhere with a cheaper alternative.

There are really only three variables at stake when a customer is considering whether to make a purchase: quality, price and timing. Put simply, the three questions are:

* Will it do the job?
* How much will it cost?
* When can I have it?

When you are negotiating, it is essential to remember that you can always have some flexibility on any two of the three variables, but never on all three. For example, you may be able to reduce the price if you are given a longer time. You may be able to do it quicker if you can charge more. And no one will ever admit to wanting low quality, but things can be short-circuited.

A good way to remember this negotiating stance is to try starting every sentence with the word 'if'. This ensures that you interrelate all the variables so that you never give all three away and end up in a pickle. For example, 'If I have to deliver it by Friday, the price will have to increase'; 'If you need the price to reduce, I will need longer to do the job.'

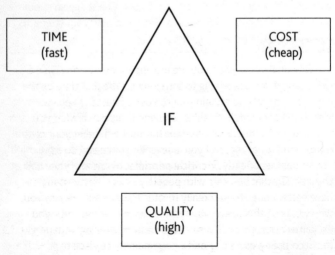

The 'if' triangle.

54 *Have a system for noting your calls*

Keep a full list of all your contacts and have a system for contacting them – use the contact list and new business hit list that we looked at in Chapter 2. Keep them right up to date. Choose an appropriate contact frequency for your business that does not represent pestering. By all means note some detail about what was said if you think you might forget, but don't clutter the list with irrelevant stuff that might impede your next call. Staying organized in this area says volumes about your reliability and efficiency.

* The appropriate timing of your call says that you are diligent but not desperate or aggressive.
* The fact that you know when you last spoke shows that you are on the ball.
* The fact that you did call back when you said you would means that you are thoroughly organized and are therefore likely to be similarly efficient when doing a job for the client.
* If you have a new idea or have noted a development in their business circumstances to which you can refer, even better.

55 *Be natural and human*

One final point when you are looking for new business, and particularly if you are talking to someone for the first time on the phone: be natural and remain true to your character. Keep your pride. Don't apologize for calling, and don't talk down what you have to offer. There is every chance that they will find your call helpful and interesting, and you'll never know unless you ask.

Remember one of the critical principles of running your own business: 'Only do business with people you like.' If they don't want to use you, it doesn't really matter. If they won't talk to you, it doesn't matter. Not everybody works with everyone else, and you will derive far more job satisfaction from working with people whose company you enjoy and who genuinely appreciate your contribution. In fact, many people leave larger companies precisely because they cannot find these qualities in their work. Therefore, there's not much point in working on your own if you simply end up replicating all the aspects of your previous working life that you were trying to change.

All you need is enough work to keep you stimulated and solvent. No adverse response is personal – it's just business. If it's not happening with a particular prospect, let it go, and keep your self-esteem intact. On the other hand, you will be jubilant when you have completed a successful call that has given you work. Then you will definitely know that you have tamed the telephone.

The ten golden rules of unsolicited calling*

1 Type out a list of people to call.
2 Print it out. If it's on the screen you won't do it.
3 Always print the phone number by the name. If you don't, you won't make the call.
4 Use a red pen to tick off your calls.
5 Never leave a message. If you do, you immediately cede control of the contact to the other person. This means that, the moment you call again, you are pestering.
6 If they are not there but someone else answers, ask for a good time to catch them, make a note, and call back. Do not be tempted to leave your name.
7 If you get voicemail, write down their mobile number and call them, or note any other information on the message and use it if appropriate.
8 When you do get through, make it sound as though it's the first time you've tried, even if it has taken weeks.
9 Make sure you can sell what you do in one sentence. Become adept at describing what you do rapidly and succinctly.
10 Always be cheerful and positive.

*Notice I have chosen not to call it 'cold-calling'. It is your job to make it warm, and the client may well welcome your call, so think positive.

Flashback

* Don't call it 'cold calling'.
* Admit that the phone will never ring unless you market yourself.
* Understand that 100 calls will get 40 meetings and three jobs.
* Prepare your selling angles.
* Do not use jargon to disguise what you do.
* Tell them you are available.
* Try selling the opposite of everyone else.
* Tell them it is simple (because you are experienced).
* Don't start discounting before you have even met.
* Have a system for noting your calls.

6

how to conduct yourself

If you behave well, then your company will be well regarded. If you come across as an idiot, disorganized, or untrustworthy, then so will your company. So keep an eye on how you conduct yourself and make sure it tallies with how you wish your company to be perceived. Chances are, if you try to guess the outcome of something, you'll be wrong as often as you are right. So stop second-guessing everything and get stuck in. All the tasks need doing, so don't distinguish between nice and nasty things to do – just get on with it. Never moan in front of customers. Nobody is interested. Take a few moments to work out whether the thing you are about to do will achieve the result you desire. If you conclude that it won't, then don't do it. Never do anything unless you know why you are doing it.

We have covered many of the emotional and practical aspects of how to run your own business. There is another utterly essential element that books cannot really teach you, but which requires careful attention nonetheless. It is not tangible. You can't buy it. You can't quantify or measure it. You may be able to acquire a few of the skills that allow you to believe that you have got 'it' about right, although you will never know for sure. So what is this elusive quality? It is how to conduct yourself.

When you work for yourself, the way that you come across is absolutely paramount. Within minutes, seconds even, you can convey completely the wrong impression. Your manners, your dress, your attitude – they all count for a great deal. They can lose the interest or respect of your potential customer in an instant. When you launch your own business, you owe it to yourself to consider very carefully what sort of image you wish to convey.

56 *You are the company culture*

You need to confront the fact that, when you work on your own, you are the company culture. There are no hazy mission statements to fall back on, no Human Resources department, and no glossy brochure to cover up for shoddy behaviour. You need to behave as you would like others to behave. What does that mean? Well, disregarding personal style for a moment, there are some basic principles of good conduct to which you should adhere. For example:
* Be polite
* Be realistic
* Turn up on time
* Return calls when you say you will
* Pay your bills immediately
* Over-deliver if you wish, but never under-deliver.

You can create your own list of this type based on your personal preferences and the nature of your business. Over time, you will undoubtedly receive back as much good behaviour as you dish out. You will gain a reputation for high standards, integrity and honesty. Repeat business will follow.

Or, put another way, if you are small-minded, you will lose good customers and attract those who are also small-minded and unreliable. At an early stage, map out what you believe to be the important parts of how to conduct your business, and use that as a blueprint to determine how you should conduct yourself, and in turn what you expect and desire of others. This will stand you in good stead if you have to confront a dilemma about whether to decline some business, or if you have to take the harsh decision to inform an existing customer that you will no longer work with them. Making such a fundamental decision on the spot often comes across as impetuousness or impatience, but if you have thought through your principles carefully, you can state calmly and clearly that their way of doing things does not tally with yours. That's your right as someone who works on their own.

57 Only do business with people that you like

This is quite a tricky area but it really is worth spending the time to work out how you feel about your business relationships. Naturally, if you work in a service business or run a retail outlet you can't vet everybody with whom you have a transaction. But you can choose the nature of your suppliers and associates. And as you develop your own personal style, you will become better at working out what other people are like to deal with. Eventually, you should be in a position whereby it is you who chooses to do business with somebody, not the other way round.

Why is this important? Because ultimately if you do not enjoy the company of the people with whom you have to interact, you will effectively have engineered a state of affairs in which you don't like what you do. This is a disaster for anyone who runs their own business. Indeed, the whole point of working on your own is to design a set-up that suits your particular style. Of course, sometimes it takes a while for someone to show their true colours, and there will be times when somebody you really like lets you down. Unfortunately, there is nothing you can do about this, and it is undoubtedly true that any disappointments will be felt harder by you as an individual than by companies in the collective sense. However, in the long run, your judgement will improve with experience, and your goal should be only to do business with the people that you like.

58 *Subsume your ego*

There is a huge difference between having a particular personal style and having a big ego. Personal style is distinctive, desirable and an important element of why people choose to do business with you. Ego is destructive, selfish and impedes business relationships. If you want to be a success, and you have a big ego, you need to have a personal truth session and bury it. This is not so that you become an automaton with no character, but so that your skills and qualities can come to the fore and be seen to be of value by potential customers without your ego detracting from them. If you are showboating all the time, this is unlikely to be the case.

It often helps if you let your customers believe or claim that many of your ideas are theirs. You will get more repeat business. If you make someone look good, they will be eternally grateful. This is not sycophancy. When you hear that someone has 'bought into' one of your ideas, it means they have joined in and helped to convince themselves of the value of it. This is outstanding selling, and cannot happen if you keep banging on about how it was 'my idea'.

Another way of reconciling this with your ego is to remember that, once a client has paid you for your work, it is actually theirs. In the case of tangible products, this is obviously self-evident. But in the grey area of ideas and advice, even the 'copyright' of your recommendations becomes your clients' property, assuming that you have negotiated an appropriate price and taken intellectual property issues into account. It should in fact be a genuine piece of flattery if a client chooses to champion your work and goes so far as to claim it as their own.

59 Do not distinguish between nice and nasty things to do

What a strange idea! It is human nature to say 'I love doing x' and 'I hate doing y'. Sadly, now that you are your own boss, you need to stop making the distinction between the two. Why? Because it was your decision to go it alone, and whatever needs doing has to be done and is ultimately entirely for your own personal benefit. Even if the task is working out how much tax to pay, it is worth doing well because if you don't, you will be the one to lose out.

It is also inaccurate to presuppose that something you expect to be nasty will actually turn out to be so. In reality, the outcome of a situation that you are anxious about is frequently the opposite of what you expect it to be. This may sound false but it is actually true. For instance, can you imagine how you might have a better meeting firing someone than giving them a pay rise? No? Have a look at these two examples.

Proof that nasty things can turn out to be nice

Employer: I'm very sorry but after a lot of discussion and anxiety I'm afraid we can't keep you in this job any longer.

Employee: I can't say I'm surprised. I haven't been coping very well and I haven't been happy. I was thinking of going travelling instead.

Proof that nice things can turn out to be nasty

Employer: I am pleased to tell you that we have agreed a £3,000 pay rise for you.

Employee: I'm really disappointed. I was expecting a minimum of £5,000.

So you see, that supposedly nasty cold-call looming on your checklist might well be the very thing that makes you most happy this month. Go on. Get to it!

60 Talk to yourself

Talking to yourself is not a sign of madness. It is actually an extremely helpful way for someone who works on their own to clarify things when no one else is around. Saying things out loud is a highly constructive thing to do. Go on, say it out loud now. You can eliminate all manner of nonsense from letters if you take the trouble to read them out loud. Frequently, they sound ludicrous when you read them back. You know the sort of thing: 'Please do not hesitate to contact myself ...' You would never speak like that, so don't write that way either.

Talking out loud also cures twaddle and jargon on presentation charts, waffle in marketing material, and spouting garbage on the telephone. If you practise your telephone pitch out loud and conclude that you sound like a twit, then that is clearly time well spent.

Another benefit of talking to yourself is that at least you are guaranteed a decent conversation and, although you may disagree with yourself, at least you won't have a flaming row! Despite what the amateur psychologists say, it's healthy, it's amusing, and for those of you poor people who miss the office, it provides a bit of banter about the place as well.

61 Remind yourself of all the positive things you have done

This is not a piece of self-delusion therapy. It is simply the knack of staying positive. All self-employed people suffer from some form of self-doubt. You don't have colleagues congratulating you on a job well done, so you need to generate your own humble form of self-congratulation. Think about it. No one else is going to bother, so you need to find a private way to celebrate your successes and keep your confidence levels up.

Consider these ideas for reminding yourself that you are actually pretty good at what you do and that you deserve a pat on the back:

* Write down your income.
* Write down your profit.

* Say out loud: 'I am still in business.'
* Choose which recent business transaction was your favourite.
* Ask a customer if they will write a reference for you.
* Ask your partner or a friend if they think you are any good at what you do.
* Invent an ingenious plan for the near future.
* Calculate whether you can afford a holiday soon.
* Book a holiday.
* If you have rivals, consider whether they are doing as well as you.

Remember this straightforward maxim:

Everything you achieve, you have done yourself

62 Never moan

Moaning is one of the most unattractive features of any personality. Whose company would you prefer? Someone with a positive, optimistic outlook or someone who spends the whole time bellyaching about things that aren't going well? Moaning is unacceptable for anyone who works on their own. Why? Because it is actually an admission of failure. If you don't agree, here is a simple translation of a moaner's conversation to illustrate the point:

Bloke in pub: 'Business is really tough at the moment and things aren't going very well.'

There are two possible translations of this remark:

'I am not talented enough to get the work I want.'

or:

'I am too lazy to get the work I need.'

This is not an exaggeration. If you run your own business, then your fortunes are entirely in your hands. You can invoke as many higher powers as you like, blame macro-economic conditions and invent reams of blether about precisely why you don't have enough work at the moment. None of this smokescreen will disguise the fact that you haven't had the wit or the determination to go and get it. This is not some assertion cooked up by a motivation guru or a sales zealot. It is cold, hard logic. So type it up and stick it on the wall: *No moaning.*

There is one other essential part of the 'No moaning' credo. Never be tempted to join in with a customer who is moaning. You can sympathize briefly, but then it is your job to suggest ways in which you can make it better, otherwise these dreadful people will rapidly turn you into a moaner too.

63 *Never drink during the day*

If this point needs clarification, go back and work for a company. This is a no-brainer. The same goes for drugs and anything else that has the capacity to turn you into a blithering idiot during work hours. Save it for the weekend! If you ever receive a call from a customer in the afternoon and you are less than compos mentis, your reputation will be on the slide immediately. 'I wouldn't use him, he's a bit of a drinker' is not how you would wish to be described around town. If you really do have to have a near-compulsory jolly with a customer one day, then turn your mobile off and return any calls when you are sober, saying that unfortunately you were in an all-day meeting or out of town. Never get involved in important business when you are in danger of talking rubbish.

64 *Never watch daytime TV*

As with drinking, watching daytime TV is the rapid road to Loserville. What makes this so obvious?
* You should be working.
* You won't learn anything.
* After a short while, your IQ will probably fall.

If you disagree with this and insist on watching this drivel, then you only have two possible courses of action:

1 Reduce the quality of your work from now on to reflect your new low-level intellect.
2 Lower your prices immediately to reflect your diminished aspirations.

65 *Never finish a day before deciding what to do the next morning*

This simple little discipline works incredibly well. It is outstandingly easy to do, and is the best ever way of ensuring a good night's sleep. Simply write down what you have to do the next day and, if appropriate, allocate the necessary time for it. Now you can relax. There are many subsidiary benefits to this approach. First, it is impossible to forget to do something because it is written down. Second, you come across as totally on the ball because you genuinely do know what you are doing the next day. And third, you don't have to worry about the tasks for the next day so you can go and have that drink after all.

66 *Never do anything unless you know why you are doing it*

How blindingly obvious is this statement? It would be a good principle for all businesspeople to abide by. Actually, it applies to anything you ever do in your whole life. This is so profoundly irrefutable that it is worth stating again:

Never do anything unless you know why you are doing it

It stands to reason. Think carefully about what you are doing and why you are doing it. Your time is your potential money. If you are doing something unnecessary, then for every minute you do so, you are shooting yourself in the foot. Only do the things that matter. Your time is too precious to approach it any other way.

67 Have reserve plans for every day

When you start out working on your own, you may well quite naïvely assume that the shape of tomorrow will be exactly as it is written in your personal organizer. Nothing could be further from the truth! Just when you have put a suit on, on a day when you think you have three meetings, they may have all been cancelled by 9.30 a.m. If that does happen, it is not acceptable to sit around and do nothing on the grounds that everything has changed. In fact, you should assume every day that everything *will* change.

Being incapable of adapting rapidly is a big warning sign for anyone who works on their own. Expressing dismay that everything has changed at short notice conveys the impression that it is easy to catch you on the hop and that you are a bit of a plodder. Life's a mess – roll with it and enjoy the ride!

You need Plans B, C and so on that you can engage immediately when all the other activities fall away. The trick to avoid disappointment is to work out that this *will* happen *before* it happens. Then when it does, which it undoubtedly will, instead of being aghast at this extraordinary development and going into a flat spin, you simply reach for your Plan B file. Relish the thought that the wonderful thing about Plan B is that Plan B is often more productive than Plan A.

Flashback

* Acknowledge that you are the company culture.
* Subsume your ego.
* Do not distinguish between nice and nasty things to do.
* Remind yourself of all the positive things you have done.
* Never moan.
* Never drink during the day.
* Never watch daytime TV.

* Never finish a day before deciding what to do the next morning.
* Never do anything unless you know why you are doing it.
* Remember that Plan B is often more productive than Plan A.

Run your own business successfully: flashback

Chapter 1

* Assume that you have something to offer.
* Be honest with yourself.
* Research your market thoroughly.
* Work out how much money you need.
* Write a simple, realistic plan.
* Invest in a distinctive identity.
* Get connected.
* Appoint a good accountant.
* Work out the materials you need.
* Network constantly without being irritating.

Chapter 2

* Write out your contact list and new business hit list.
* Write down everyone you want to get in touch with.
* Put the phone number by every one of them.
* Do everything when you think of it.
* Constantly review the list to see if you are being realistic.
* Keep the numbers manageable.
* Keep inventing new ideas for contacting someone.
* Every time you get through to someone, move them to your contact list.
* Try to have 20–30 meetings fixed for the next 4–6 weeks.
* Never cancel a new business meeting because you are 'too busy'.

Chapter 3

* Concentrate on the money, but do not become obsessed with it.
* Weigh up the Service v Product distinction.
* Work out how to have a near-infinite margin.
* Consider the lucky seven money questions.
* Try to avoid the most time-consuming issue ever: other people.
* Try to sell what you do, more so than materials with a mark up.
* Examine the price–quality equation: if you cost a lot, you must be good.
* Do not be small-minded about money.
* Be canny about requests for free or 'win only' work.
* Consider Everyday Flexible Pricing.

Chapter 4

* Choose the right method of communicating.
* Become adept at describing what you do in less than 30 seconds.
* Be prepared to improvise on the spot.
* Introduce some humanity into your CV.
* Remember that people give business to those with whom they like having meetings.
* Meet lots of people and stay open-minded.
* Take your customers to lunch and insist on paying.
* Rewrite all your marketing materials.
* Design a clever mailing to send to your customers.
* Ask your customers what else you could do for them.

Chapter 5

* Don't' call it 'cold calling'.
* Admit that the phone will never ring unless you market yourself.
* Understand that 100 calls will get 40 meetings and three jobs.
* Prepare your selling angles.
* Do not use jargon to disguise what you do.
* Tell them you are available.
* Try selling the opposite of everyone else.
* Tell them it is simple (because you are experienced).
* Don't start discounting before you have even met.
* Have a system for noting your calls.

Chapter 6

* Acknowledge that you are the company culture.
* Subsume your ego.
* Do not distinguish between nice and nasty things to do.
* Remind yourself of all the positive things you have done.
* Never moan.
* Never drink during the day.
* Never watch daytime TV.
* Never finish a day before deciding what to do the next morning.
* Never do anything unless you know why you are doing it.
* Remember that Plan B is often more productive than Plan A.